EX · LIBRIS

GENERAL MAP
OF
THE WORLD

Mary Parkinson

For
Mother with
Love

For Mother with Love

Edited by Grace Hudson

Designed by Liz Trovato

GRAMERCY BOOKS
NEW YORK · AVENEL

Introduction and compilation
Copyright © 1995 by
Random House Value Publishing, Inc.
All rights reserved

This edition is published by Gramercy Books,
distributed by Random House Value Publishing, Inc.
40 Engelhard Avenue
Avenel, New Jersey 07001

Random House
New York • Toronto • London • Sydney • Auckland

Printed and bound in the United States of America

Library of Congress Cataloging-in-Publication Data
For mother with love.
p. cm.
ISBN 0-517-12246-4
1. Mothers—Literary collections. I. Gramercy Books (Firm)
PN6071.M7F67 1995
808.8'0085'2—dc20   94-40659
                                             CIP

8 7 6 5 4 3 2 1

INTRODUCTION

Novelists and dramatists, poets and painters have always been inspired by the relationship of mother and child. Many of the world's outstanding leaders in every field of endeavor have heaped praise on their own mothers and have acknowledged with pride their lifelong influence. In memorable words and evocative images, *For Mother With Love* pays tribute to mothers and to motherhood.

D. H. Lawrence, for example, describes his mother as "my first, great love," and Strickland Gillilan says that no one can be wealthier than he, since "I had a mother who read to me." James M. Barrie writes: "When you looked into my mother's eyes you knew, as if He told you, why God sent her into the world—it was to open the minds of all who looked to beautiful thoughts."

Pearl Buck, Henry Ward Beecher, Washington Irving, Honoré de Balzac, Oliver Wendell Holmes, and George Eliot are among the many who extol motherhood. Luree Miller states, "While others strive to compete, mothers work to hold the world together." Kate Douglas Wiggin compares maternal love to an orange tree that "buds and blossoms and bears all at once." According to an Indian proverb, "A mother exceeds a thousand fathers in the right to reverence." And Florida Scott-Maxwell says, "No matter how old a mother is she watches her middle-aged children for signs of improvement."

Included, too, are women's descriptions of their own experiences of motherhood and of the poignancy of being a mother. Agatha Christie, for example, declares that "there is nothing more thrilling in this world, I think, than having a child that is yours, and yet is mysteriously a stranger." And Alice Duer Miller writes that on the spring morning her son was born, "hope was born—the future lived again."

This celebration of mothers is made all the more delightful by the lovely decorations and illustrations that complement the words. Among the artists represented are Jessie Willcox Smith, Harrison Fisher, Kate Greenaway, and W. L. Taylor.

Compiled and designed to be a gift of love, this enchanting book will surely be enjoyed and treasured by every mother and every grown-up child.

GRACE HUDSON

New York

1995

When each of her own three children was on the way, Mother would say to those closest to her, "I don't know whether this will be a boy or a girl, and I don't care. But this child was invited into the world and it will be a wonderful child."

MARGARET BOURKE-WHITE,
TWENTIETH-CENTURY PIONEER IN PHOTOGRAPHY
AND PHOTOJOURNALISM

*I*n the sheltered
simplicity of the first days
after a baby is born,
one sees again the
magical closed circle,
the miraculous sense of
two people existing
only for each other.

ANN MORROW LINDBERGH,
TWENTIETH-CENTURY AMERICAN WRITER

Maternal love, like an orange tree, buds and blossoms and bears at once. When a woman puts her finger for the first time into the tiny hand of her baby and feels that helpless clutch which tightens her very heartstrings, she is born again with the newborn child.

KATE DOUGLAS WIGGIN (1856-1923),
AMERICAN WRITER AND EDUCATOR

Children are what the mothers are,

No fondest father's fondest care

Can fashion so the infant heart

As those creative beams that dart,

With all their hopes and fears, upon

The cradle of a sleeping son.

WALTER SAVAGE LANDOR,
ENGLISH POET AND PROSE WRITER,
WHOSE WORK SPANNED THE EIGHTEENTH
AND NINETEENTH CENTURIES

Just a little baby lying in my arms,

Would that I could keep you with your baby charms;

Helpless, clinging fingers; downy, golden hair,

Where the sunshine lingers, caught from otherwhere;

Roly-poly shoulders, dimple in your cheek;

Dainty little blossom, in a world of woe;

This I fain would keep you, for I love you so.

LOUISE CHANDLER MOULTON (1835-1908),
AMERICAN POET

Out of the dark, and dearth

Of happiness on earth,

Out of a world inured to

   death and pain;

On a fair spring morn

To me a son was born,

And hope was born—the future

   lived again.

To me a son was born,

The lonely hard forlorn

Travail was, as the Bible

   tells, forgot.

How old, how commonplace

To look upon the face

Of your first-born, and glory

    in your lot.

To know the reason why

Buds blow, and blossoms die,

Why beauty fades, and genius

    is undone,

And how unjustified

Is any human pride

In all creation—save in this

    common one.

ALICE DUER MILLER,
TWENTIETH-CENTURY AMERICAN WRITER

The God to whom

little boys say their prayers has a face

very like their mother's.

J. M. BARRIE (1860-1937),
SCOTTISH NOVELIST AND DRAMATIST

*I*n the Heavens above,

The angels, whispering

to one another,

Can find, among their burning

terms of love,

None so devotional as that

of "mother."

EDGAR ALLAN POE,
NINETEENTH-CENTURY AMERICAN WRITER

A Mother exceeds
a thousand fathers in the
right to reverence.

INDIAN PROVERB

Mother is the

name for God in the lips and

hearts of children.

WILLIAM MAKEPEACE THACKERAY (1811-1863),

ENGLISH NOVELIST

No rubies of red for my lady,

  No jewel that glitters and charms;

But the light of the skies,

In a little one's eyes,

  And a necklace of two little arms.

Of two little arms that are clinging,

  (Oh ne'er was a necklace like this!)

And the wealth of the world,

And love's sweetness impearled,

  In the joy of a little one's kiss.

A necklace of love for my lady,

  That was linked by the angels above,

No other but this,

And a tender, sweet kiss,

  That sealeth a little one's love.

FRANK L. STANTON (1857-1927),
AMERICAN POET AND JOURNALIST

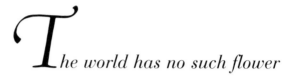

The world has no such flower

in any land,

And no such pearl in any gulf

in the sea,

As any babe on any mother's knee.

ALGERNON SWINBURNE,
NINETEENTH-CENTURY BRITISH POET

MOTHER AND CHILD

There is nothing more

thrilling in this world, I think,

than having a child that is yours, and

yet is mysteriously a stranger.

AGATHA CHRISTIE (1890-1976),
ENGLISH WRITER

E WILLCOX SMITH.

M y mother was the most perfect and magnetic character, the rarest combination of practical, moral, and spiritual, and the least selfish, of all and any I have ever known, and by me O so much the most deeply loved.

WALT WHITMAN,
NINETEENTH-CENTURY AMERICAN POET

Who ran to help me when I fell,

And would some pretty story tell,

Or kiss the place to make it well?

My mother!

JANE TAYLOR (1783-1824),
ENGLISH WRITER

To be a mother is the grandest vocation in the
world. No being has a position of such power and
influence. She holds in her hands the destiny of nations;
for to her is necessarily committed the making of the
nation's citizens.

HANNAH WHITALL SMITH (1832-1911),
AMERICAN RELIGIOUS LEADER

A Mother's
love grows by giving.

CHARLES LAMB (1775-1834),
ENGLISH ESSAYIST AND CRITIC

There never was a child

so lovely but his mother was glad

to get him asleep.

RALPH WALDO EMERSON,
NINETEENTH-CENTURY AMERICAN WRITER
AND PHILOSOPHER

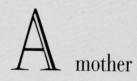

A mother

understands what

a child does not say.

JEWISH PROVERB

Aunt Eleanor wears such diamonds!

  Shiny and gay and grand,

Some on her neck and some in her hair,

  And some on her pretty hand.

One day I asked my mamma

  Why she never wore them, too;

She laughed and said, as she kissed my eyes,

  "My jewels are here, bright blue.

They laugh and dance and beam and smile,

  So lovely all the day,

And never like Aunt Eleanor's go

  In a velvet box to stay.

Hers are prisoned in bands of gold,

  But mine are free as air,

Set in a bonny, dimpled face,

  And shadowed with shining hair!

EUGENE FIELD,
NINETEENTH-CENTURY AMERICAN
NEWSPAPERMAN AND POET

During the nineteen thirties when I was in high school, my mother went back to college to take art classes five days a week at the University of Washington.

More and more often, in the afternoon, we found Mother in the basement sculpting instead of in the kitchen cooking. My father did more of the grocery shopping and often cooked our dinners. "Your mother," he explained, "is coming into full bloom."

LUREE MILLER,
TWENTIETH-CENTURY AMERICAN WRITER

*S*ometimes the strength

of motherhood is greater than

natural laws.

BARBARA KINGSOLVER,
TWENTIETH-CENTURY AMERICAN WRITER

It seems to me that my mother was the most splendid woman I ever knew.... If I have amounted to anything, it will be due to her.

CHARLES CHAPLIN,
TWENTIETH-CENTURY
FILM ACTOR AND PRODUCER

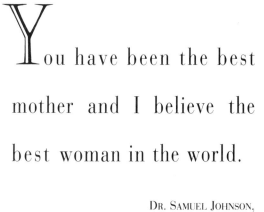

You have been the best
mother and I believe the
best woman in the world.

DR. SAMUEL JOHNSON,
EIGHTEENTH-CENTURY ENGLISH LEXICOGRAPHER,
CRITIC, AND CONVERSATIONALIST

You may have tangible wealth untold;

Caskets of jewels and coffers of gold.

Richer than I you can never be—

I had a mother who read to me.

STRICKLAND GILLILAN,
AMERICAN PUBLICIST AND POET,
WHOSE WORK SPANNED THE NINETEENTH
AND TWENTIETH CENTURIES

M ost
mothers are instinctive
philosophers.

HARRIET BEECHER STOWE,
NINETEENTH-CENTURY AMERICAN WRITER

Motherhood is an honorable profession that has fallen on hard times. These days mothers tend to be much maligned. As the trend toward specialization and professionalization accelerates, they are becoming an endangered species: old-fashioned generalists who make the time and take the trouble to act on humanistic values. While others strive to compete, mothers work to hold the world together.

LUREE MILLER,
TWENTIETH-CENTURY
AMERICAN WRITER

A man who has been
the indisputable favorite of
his mother keeps for life the
feeling of a conqueror, that
confidence of success that often
induces real success.

SIGMUND FREUD (1856-1939),
AUSTRIAN NEUROLOGIST AND THE FATHER
OF PSYCHOANALYSIS

With a mother of different mental caliber I probably would have turned out badly.

THOMAS ALVA EDISON,
AMERICAN INVENTOR ABOUT HIS MOTHER,
NANCY ELLIOTT EDISON

M y mother always

seemed to me a fairy princess,

a radiant being possessed of

limitless riches and power. . . .

WINSTON CHURCHILL,
BRITISH STATESMAN AND PRIME MINISTER

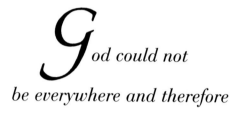

$\mathcal{G}$od could not

be everywhere and therefore

made mothers.

JEWISH PROVERB

Up the stairs very gently we creep,

At the door very softly we knock,

And we wonder if Mother's asleep

(We were dressed before seven o'clock).

If she thinks it's the letters or tea

What a splendid surprise it will be!

For it's only the children—it's us,

Who are standing outside at her door.

There is Sylvia and Peggy, and Gus,

We three, and the baby makes four—

And we're bringing her flowers to say

"Many happy returns of the day!"

GITHA SOWERBY,
NINETEENTH-CENTURY AUTHOR
OF POEMS AND STORIES FOR CHILDREN

The mother's heart
is the child's schoolroom.

HENRY WARD BEECHER (1813-1887),
AMERICAN CLERGYMAN

*The heart of a mother is a
deep abyss at the bottom of which
you will always discover forgiveness.*

HONORÉ DE BALZAC,
NINETEENTH-CENTURY FRENCH NOVELIST

O f all your endless acts and words of love,

never was any so dear to me as your last

letter;—so generous, so sweet, so holy! What on

earth is so precious as a mother's love; and who has

a mother like mine!

MARGARET FULLER (1810-1850),
AMERICAN JOURNALIST

My Dear Little Daughter,

You are not really so little as all that, I know, since you have just had your eighteenth birthday. . . . But, like all real mothers since the world began, I still think of you as little: and the sweetest thing that God ever made. . . . When I say a real mother, I obviously don't mean a good mother: I mean a mother who, however bad she is, puts her young fiercely before everything else. Whose love for them is not the sentimental thing that civilized love suggests; but more like the possessive fury of a beast in the jungle with a potent element of wonder thrown in: wonder at her production of them.

CAITLIN THOMAS,
WELSH WRITER AND THE WIDOW
OF THE POET DYLAN THOMAS

When God thought of MOTHER, He must have laughed with satisfaction and framed it quickly, so rich, so deep, so divine, so full of soul, power and beauty was the conception.

HENRY WARD BEECHER (1813-1887),
AMERICAN CLERGYMAN

Always a "little boy" to her,

No matter how old he's grown,

Her eyes are blind to the strands of gray,

She's deaf to his manly tone.

His voice is the same as the day he asked,

"What makes the old cat purr?"

Ever and ever he's just the same—

A little boy to her.

Always a "little boy" to her,

And to him she's the mother fair,

With the laughing eyes and the cheering smile

Of the boyhood days back there.

Back there, somewhere in the midst of years—

Back there with the childish joy,

And to her he is never the man we see,

But always her "little boy."

AUTHOR UNKNOWN

My mother was a great reader, and with ten minutes to spare before the starch was ready would begin the "Decline and Fall"— and finish it, too, that winter....Biography and exploration were her favorite reading, for choice the biography of men who had been good to their mothers, and she liked the explorers to be alive so that she could shudder at the thought of their venturing forth again, but though she expressed a hope that they would have the sense to stay at home henceforth, she gleamed with admiration when they disappointed her. In later days I had a friend who was an African explorer, and she was in two minds about him; he was one of the more engrossing of mortals to her, she admired him

prodigiously, pictured him at the head of his cara-

van, now attacked by savages, now by wild

beasts, and adored him for the uneasy hours he

gave her, but she was also afraid that he wanted to

take me with him, and then she thought he should

be put down by law.

Explorers' mothers also interested her very much; the books might tell her nothing about them, but she could create them for herself and wring her hands in sympathy with them when they had got no news of him for six months. Yet there were times when she grudged him to them—as the day when he returned victorious. Then what was before her eyes was not the son coming marching home again but an old woman peering for him round the window curtain and trying not to look up-lifted. The newspaper reports would be about the son, but my mother's comment was "She's a proud woman this night."

J. M. BARRIE
IN HIS BIOGRAPHY OF HIS MOTHER,
MARGARET OGILVY

Some are kissing mothers

and some are scolding mothers,

but it is love just the same, and

most mothers kiss and scold

together.

PEARL S. BUCK,

TWENTIETH-CENTURY AMERICAN NOVELIST

J ust as the ripe fruit breaks off from the tree, so a time will come when you will have to break off from your mother. It's sad—sad for me too. But it's something to be glad about for your sake, since it means that you are growing up.

ISOKO HATANO,
FROM A LETTER OF APRIL 1948
TO HER SON, ICHIRO

Let me not forget that I am the daughter of a woman who bent her head, trembling, between the blades of a cactus, her wrinkled face full of ecstasy over the promise of a flower, a woman who herself never ceased to flower, untiringly, during three-quarters of a century.

SIDONIE-GABRIELLE COLETTE (1873-1954),
FRENCH NOVELIST, CRITIC, AND JOURNALIST

She openeth her mouth with wisdom; and in her tongue is the law of kindness. She looketh well to the ways of her household. And eateth not the bread of idleness. Her children arise up, and call her blessed; her husband also, and he praiseth her.

PROVERBS 31:26-28

In the man whose childhood

has known caresses there lies a

fiber of memory which can be

touched to noble issues.

GEORGE ELIOT,
NINETEENTH-CENTURY
ENGLISH NOVELIST

A father may turn his back on his child, brothers and sisters may become inveterate enemies, husbands may desert their wives; wives, their husbands; but a mother's love endures, through all, in good repute, in bad repute, in the face of the world's condemnation, a mother still loves on and still hopes that her child may turn from his evil ways and repent; still she remembers the infant smiles that once filled her bosom with rapture, the merry laugh, the joyful shout of his childhood, the opening promise of his youth; and she can never be brought to think him all unworthy.

WASHINGTON IRVING (1783-1859),
AMERICAN WRITER

M others are the only
goddesses in whom the whole
world believes.

ANONYMOUS

Osborne, May 26, 1858

On the afternoon of my birthday (which was a wet one) I received your dear letter of the 22nd with such dear, warm, hearty expressions of love and affection for which 1000 thanks. I have no doubt dearest child that you can now much better appreciate Mama's love and affection and understand how all that you grumbled and struggled and kicked against was for your good, and meant in love!—your love and affection you know, dearest child, I never doubted, I only was often grieved and hurt at your manner, your temper.

QUEEN VICTORIA,
IN A LETTER TO HER DAUGHTER

$\mathcal{N}$o matter how old a mother is

she watches her middle-aged children

for signs of improvement.

FLORIDA SCOTT-MAXWELL,
TWENTIETH-CENTURY AMERICAN WRITER

All that I am
or hope to be I owe to my
angel mother.

ABRAHAM LINCOLN,
SIXTEENTH PRESIDENT OF THE UNITED STATES

In afterlife you may have friends, fond, dear friends, but never will you have again the inexpressible love and gentleness lavished upon you which none but a Mother bestowes.

THOMAS BABINGTON MACAULAY,
NINETEENTH-CENTURY ENGLISH HISTORIAN,
AUTHOR, AND STATESMAN

So if I do not seem happy with the thought of you—you will understand. I must feel my mother's hand slip out of mine before I can really take yours. She is my first, great love. She was a wonderful, rare woman—you do not know; as strong, and steadfast, and generous as the sun. She could be as swift as a white whiplash, and as kind and gentle as warm rain, and as steadfast as the irreducible earth beneath us.

D. H. LAWRENCE (1855-1930),
IN A LETTER HE WROTE IN DECEMBER 1910
TO LOUIE BURROWS, THE WOMAN TO WHOM HE
HAD PROPOSED A FEW DAYS EARLIER

Youth fades; love droops;

the leaves of friendship fall;

A mother's secret hope outlives

them all!

OLIVER WENDELL HOLMES,
NINETEENTH-CENTURY AMERICAN MAN OF LETTERS

Backward, turn backward, O time, in your flight,

Make me a child again, just for tonight!

Mother, come back from the echoless shore,

Take me again to your heart as of yore;

Kiss from my forehead the furrows of care,

Smooth the few silver threads out of my hair;

Over my slumbers your loving watch keep;

Rock me to sleep, Mother, rock me to sleep!

ELIZABETH AKERS ALLEN,
NINETEENTH-CENTURY AMERICAN POET

When you looked into my mother's eyes you knew, as if He told you, why God sent her into the world—it was to open the minds of all who looked to beautiful thoughts. And that is the beginning and end of literature. Those eyes guided me through life, and I pray God they may remain my only earthly judge to the last. They were never more my guide than when I helped to put her to earth, not whimpering because my mother had been taken away after seventy-six glorious years of life, but exulting in her even at the grave.

J. M. BARRIE
IN HIS BIOGRAPHY OF HIS MOTHER,
MARGARET OGILVY